FINISHING LINE PRESS

www.finishinglinepress.com

postcards from glasshouse drive

poems by

Woody Woodger

Finishing Line Press
Georgetown, Kentucky

postcards from glasshouse drive

ACKNOWLEDGMENTS

as big a hug as my skinny little arms can manage for the readers and editors of
the following journals where some of these poems have previously appeared,
many in earlier forms:

2 Bridges Review
(b)OINK Zine
Soundings East
rinky dink press
Lost Tower Publications
Sigma Tau Delta Mind Murals
Postcards Poems and Prose
Every Pigeon

Publisher: Leah Maines

Editor: Christen Kincaid

Cover Art: Elizabeth Ann

Author Photo: Elizabeth Ann

Cover Design: Elizabeth Maines McCleavy

Printed in the USA on acid-free paper.
Order online: www.finishinglinepress.com
            also available on amazon.com

Author inquiries and mail orders:
Finishing Line Press
P. O. Box 1626
Georgetown, Kentucky 40324
U. S. A.

Table of Contents

for my family (and kent) & Elizabeth

on our way to your cousin's closed casket i thought

the church street
bell was suddenly a psalm

winching our air,
even through that crack snailing
down its ribs.

today is arthritis,

like a fisherman's knot
dragging through

my metacarpals—
fiber thin trails
a crab belly leaves

after low tide.

driving to work, i come across

two road signs taking a stroll down
Glasshouse toward the bridge.

they've got neanderthal brows
as they brace against this January
morning. the river's copper cogs

move under the ice sheet. these signs
must be married, i think.
i see them grumble about their drafty
skylight back home
and the misery of a half-painted

garage. she turns to him and asks
what he wants to do with dad
now that her mom's gone.

they share a criminal cigarette,
their only habit left over from the 80's,
besides Tiger Balm. i flick

my own out the car window. i'll let
the radio breathe. let the wind
dizzy this cross i've left noosed

to my rear-view since the dealership.
every uncut ounce of decency
i've prayed for comes as road salt
crashing against my windshield.

i have my uncle's brain—i instinctively
know the lethal dose of any liquid. trouble

with me is what i know has never scared me.
trouble with road salt is it seeps
into our groundwater where no angel,

no court order could ever hope to reach,
save us from ourselves.

[local funeral home, 673 glasshouse drive]

reading your cousin's
          eulogy must taste
like the chromy
          wax over a Russell

Stover. the brittle
          rubber taste
angles harvests
          from those skid marks

leading to the birch
          he scalped—a white cross
kneeling
          at its toes. all this quiet
carnage lulled

          by a dry,
creaseless breeze.

moonshine jar

dad fishes it out
of the October slurry
molting around

our barn. the thing thinks
it's a prince sitting on our dinner

table. it had to be

cleaned with a pillowcase—
that old marbled
one with spit stains

and stretch marks—

we keep as a rag
under the sink

next to a bottle of Zout.

apparently, the jar's priceless.
dad calls it *Antique*

Roadshow, collector's

cat-nip, our little lotto
from god. i think
it's a *vase deflowered.*

a confession

when your cousin came home the first thing we did was shoot up

and, like always, i felt a sputtering angel
      wench two meat hooks between my skin and nerves,

hoist me by my oily soul up to the blind spot
    right between the ceiling
                    and the crowns of our heads.

[another 23 yr old in the berkshire eagle obituaries:
cause of death unspecified]

on my last day i boil a cotton
cream *brûlée* in my oldest spoon.
the neck is sooty and cricked
like a bucked-toothed vertebrae.
there's a baby that just never
stops screaming through
the drywall. i think
some mother swaddled it, left
it to play a game of Moses.
existentially, i'm the napkin to soak
up the soda spill. there's my doorbell.
it always sounds like church
on Betamax. the dime novel
brown in my carpet has evolved
into a plague and every Thursday
your cousin takes out his coffee teeth,
gives me the business.
he says my hair looks taped
to my skull. he says the Plymouth
shoreline is a snake's
nictitating membrane stretched
over a motel window. i don't know
about that. i know i'm the new Plath—
i eat Narcan like air. my rib cage feels
like it's been soaking in Diet Coke
since June. my voice like panties
burnt by the dryer. i've been down
to my toes for a month
and i excavate the couch for coins,
saltines, condoms. i actually find
a lollipop which reminds
me of that time i watched
a kid eat his lolly-pop on the shoulder
of I-90. as he looked it over

it became a cherry monocle
to make the whole
world Robitussin queasy.
i thought he couldn't stand closer
to the highway if he wanted.
i saw all the cars knew it.

what we walk on

seashells are a main ingredient
in cape cod concrete.

think of the clammy popcorn
kernels wedged

in a pelican's gums.
i learned from NatGeo

that male pelicans will actually give
these kernels to mates

as if they were rings,
because they're sharp and opal.

females are smarter. they repurpose
the rings as oyster shuckers.

[of the end i will soon be met]

under the Edgartown
        porch light

        my wicker chair
is gagged, each joint

tied with dried
        tea strings

        and uncomfortable;
like the sail boat

with a cricked neck
        on the dock. the one

        our neighbors abandon
when fall comes. that gray

crayon over the east,
        stumbling out

        from wherever air
is packaged,

from iron and god's
        kitchen counter—

        a slurry of coupons
and wasted tulips

after the voles found the bulbs.

upon seeing my gramps in photos

i feel the squirrelly itch
from one of his peppermints
clatter behind my bicuspids—
a chisel's echo
chunking out through
my nostrils. the chisel wants
to divine the word *wheel*
out of my enamel. coincidentally,
stones and god
share a melting point.

in my kitchen i shiver against my manorexia and
contemplate mortality

it's unsleepable Tuesday

and i eat an apple

over the sink.   tonight,
                       every molecule of air

                       grew mandibles.

                       they almost teach
                 my skin the meaning

of *constellation*

                       as they teethe pink
              welts into my forearms.
                       i'd itch them off,
                       but tonight i'm too busy

wondering what sinewy
                       havoc purrs—coiled
and lipless—at the bottom

                 of my drain.

upon giving my uncle some home to come back to (i know
alcoholism's not heroin, but still)

i found my uncle's Escorts
under some saltines
in a warbling christmas tin,
the snowman's face around the rim
with the poppyseed eyes
of a Florida-bred cockroach.
once, me and mom actually
trapped one in a wine glass
on the kitchen floor. its back
was staple-bound fingernails.
when it stopped thrashing
i swore it looked
like one of those rubber replicas
field trip chaperones
have to keep the weepy boy
from seeing in the museum gift
shop. that boy's normally me.
our Shawshanked roach
stayed as patient as mom's voice
when pest control finally
picked up, the phone cord
pythoning her knuckle,
and my knees numbed
on the laminate. our prisoner
didn't give us any trouble.
pest control said it stood
so still because it knew
that if it waited long enough,
at least a few males from his clutch
in the baseboard would storm
our carpet—pale hatchlings
in a loose platoon to rescue
their father. pry him free
through jail bars. like so much rope,

their hands. the father's
and his sons' knotted like two grinless
aircraft carriers, no taller than the ankle
of some gray, sighing horizon.

ekphrastic we gave to duane michals' "the annunciation",
peabody essex salem mass

there's a limestone angel
jutting out of my town's
harbor graveyard, her robe
and sandals bleary under
the shade of a handsy willow.
she leans over a cursive Ruth
you have to dig out with paper
and charcoal. her wings
are vacuum sealed to the stone,
but her outstretched arm
is still crabbing with an index
and thumb. i heard a sailor say
she's a child, pruning the thumbtack
sun off a cork wall.

i like thinking she's a house
wife trying to prick
at god's rear end, beaming
red when he squeals.

fatigues

do you remember
when we were all boys
and your dad
would smile,
toss his white

undershirt
over your cousin's head
while he redressed
for work?
you ever figure out the smell?

musty and crisp
as a casket flag.

wondering if you remember hearing about a vietnamese summer,
springfield mass

       a girl sat in front of cartoons
       to learn English.

       bonsai trees and   Jesus posters.
                    we watch her pull at her skirt,

taking off the pixie-dust   sequins before
the washer could.

she asked, but her mom said a cold

       hose will have to do
       instead of the pool.

i can't remember if we found it funny or sad, but remember
how she watched
so much TV that she thought   birds
                 really could have hands—

       their wings, she thought, could bloom into bony palms
       if she tossed

           them pebbles.

dear customer:

that's what it says on dad's L.L.Bean gift card
tucked in our plastic christmas tree.

he says that would make a good poem
for me to write, the Glenmorangie and carols
rolling over his knee laced with used

scotch-tape. something about consumerism he wants.

and it should be long too.
i could be the one to write it, but if not me

he says, someone at least. someone should.

[thinking upon your cousin's nightmare from apartment complex b: 48 glasshouse drive]

the room that's always filing
papers has stopped
for a moment to tend and hush
her baby boy—
his stomach distended with frosted
animal crackers
and Mucinex.
the terracotta cars in the back
parking lot stand spread-
legged and sparse,
like men at the urinal.
the moon is made of god's
leftover keratin—a tungsten curse
weak and drowned out
by blue halogens
powdering the lawn.

now wondering if you remember those tobacco pickers,
southwick mass

a plaque crusted moon

to farm under. their baby slung
            over her mom's shoulder
                                    like a rifle.

she'd teethe

            on her mom's fish hook shirt tag,
            her snore

like fresh poppies.

                        she'd thankfully
            sleep by 6. always. we never

met another kid who could do that.

you said she was a gas cap
                                    purring

    as she used a whole palm to shake

your fingertip.

            they shored
                    the leaves into hip
baskets.

            all these clippings, they said,
                    to be in
California by

            Wednesday.

[upon your cousin's last ride over the zakim: april 15, 2013]

the seven of us, all hamster huddled
        in the car, we Lego linked
our knees in the backseat
        as we saw the city slip in and out,
between the lattice tension wires.

from this vantage,
        every tower juts up, military spine
and skin, eczema clay.
        your cousin said he never thought
he'd live long enough see Boston
        turn into Afghanistan.

but that day i thought the city
        was a Stonehenge
still not comfortable
        with the fog—feline and dirty—
passing souls around its feet.

the first time i wished that photo of mary could come off
the mantel

the paper says a boy and his dog found a body
        in a black trash bag buried
under the Pepperell pine-needles—
        shavings from the last hunk of copper
in the state. the dog took an exposed corner,
        pulled like it was one of his toys
and monoxide spilled like a swampy bourbon
        dad used to anoint the lip of my sippy
cup with. the boy and the dog just left
        the body there. really, what were they
supposed to do? even if the boy had an EpiPen
        full of holy water and Adderall,
i think the body might have just run to the nearest
        river, searched the reeds to find baby Moses,
drown him before his faith does.

lawn flamingo

i have no compassion for the lawn flamingo and its Miami-
colored smirk—a chassis soaked in nail polish. it just limps

forever toward the road. basement wire kneecaps and Vegas pink.
bottom-feeder, it sifts for shrimp

through the winter fertilizer. it's a seashell clock on clearance,
a plastic martini glass. in a few years, it'll tell its kids—cigarette

dangling from it beak—that they should dream to sell insurance
with a comb over or hold up signs at a boxing match. it's actually
    shameful

to watch it preen. like seeing mom do the dishes with her fingernails,
careful not to splash the wood-paneling. half way between

the splits and stepping, it's embarrassed to remember the vole
has become its only predator. gators couldn't be bothered. i could imagine

a lab-coat dissecting one specimen's leg bone, remarking
on how flat they look from either side.

[upon entering your cousin's foreclosed house]

dad warned me about the light bulb glass piled at the door, under
the side table right when you walk in. no filament, no ribbing.
just a collapsed sugar cube. a carpal flown through the food
processor. i know each time i open the door, a shard or two will
break from the pile faint as sawgrass pollen. most of these will
travel as vaporized razor blades down between my bronchioles,
but some will catch over my uvula on their way—maybe
mistaking it for a tire swing, the roof of my mouth a gummy
willow that should barely hold a robin.

[along the lines of a revelation]

your cousin taught me the purest talent—peeling an orange
              so it's skin   comes off as one sheet.
flattened, the goosey flesh   always spreads
into the Rorschach test   of an angel on the counter.

in our kitchen, proverbs hung
by clawed feet between pans and ladles.   before they went
to get your cousin's license, his dad

held some beach sand   in his palm, let the breeze take it off

toward the ocean. *that's how i'll spread your ashes,* his dad said.
for some reason,   that was your cousin's favorite story.

a confession—two months ago, my condolence letter
            for your cousin could've   fit in a Tweet.

I can feel myself growing into that cottage cheesy section

of your waist where   the button won't reach
anymore. all joy still feels like drips from the roof tarp,
          landing like god's cold thumb on your forehead.

late last summer after work

my coworker found
          a dragonfly petrified
in a case of oranges
that came in from the Cape last Monday.

     each leg dehydrated
and shivering into
          its chest.   it looked

          like a collectible nestled
in a black frame—

          bobby-pin crucified.

     the eyes were igneous,
          or licorice.   no, recklessly blue.

maybe replacements for a taxidermist
when he needs to fill in a bird's

eye sockets. plant the eyes like seeds

and watch their roots lace,
claw down toward the rain.

listening to npr after a long talk with your cousin in a taco bell

your cousin taped the menthol
he sucked to a pill
through the cracked window
and out into the turkey grease
parking lot. the smoke and ash
tumbled over the windshield,
squeegeed carcinogens
into the wiper streaks
suddenly apparent under
those blue lamps. his cigarettes
would grappled so tight
to my sinus infection, i'd smell
them when i got back home
to fold my shirts and jeans.
what about his voice made it so easy
to get lodged in your amygdala,
like the stray cork of a pop gun?
now, that makes me remember
the small boy in Worcester
Terry Gross said was holding
a bouquet of grass before
some Chevy Cruze they'll never
catch mistook him for another
junk-mule in Keds. in layman's
terms, i'm a glass jaw leaning
over the table, saying
here—right here—spiral arm
of some purple, noseless deity,
shatter my slim mouth and envy
at the odd grace of flesh.

I should just say what I mean—

there's a fist knocking
from the uncarpeted trunk of my prayers.

I don't want to tell you,

but I've learned to know there's no human
in there. Once this seizure stops pounding

I'll hoist out it's leftover flesh. And I won't
snivel like normal. I'll be good

and throw its fading warmness

to the teethy pines by the road. Sometimes
I'll remind myself there's no honor

in actually knowing how a dead bird

feels in your palm. If anyone
cares, it weighs

the exact same as the stuffed ones

in a glass case. It feels just like this oily
Nantucket dusk, the one i'm writing

an unremarkable ode to. An ode

that can't yet admit how it smells
a sleepy apocalypse stirring underneath

the earth's loosening floor boards.

Notes

driving to work, i come across is for Leah Nielsen

what we walk on is for Elizabeth Ann

[of the end i will soon be met] is for Keith Leonard and Lias Mangini.

upon giving my uncle some home to come back to (i know alcoholism's not heroin, but still) is for uncle kent.

ekphrastic we gave to duane michals' "the annunciation", peabody essex salem mass is for Robbie Auld.

dear customer: is for Marshal Scott Woodger.

[upon your cousin's last ride over the zakim: april 15, 2013] is for Joshua M. Loell.

Additional Acknowledgments

thank you to Christen Kincaid and the tireless staff at Finishing Line Press.

to the incomparable Leah Nielsen, i owe an arm, a leg, my second shin, a liver, and maybe a pinch of my immune system when science finally gets its act together. i'd also like to thank everyone in my Chapbook Writing class for struggling through the early drafts of this book as well as the rest of the Westfield State University faculty. y'all are the real heroes. to J.D. Scrimgeour and all the (Sexy) Salem State Poets 2k15, I owe you a debt of gratitude that i'll spend a lifetime paying back.

thank you to Dan Rattelle for being my own personal editor, pro bono.

thank you to my mom and dad for some reason trusting me to get a degree in poetry, to you Brad, to you uncle Brad, and to you grandma for all your love and courage. thank you too uncle kent. i hope you read this with some fritos and gin.

and finally, thank you to my most gentle editor, my personal photographer, my deepest love, and my dearest friend, Elizabeth Ann. i love you.

W oody Woodger's poetry has received publication in *Prairie Margins, Barely South, Exposition Review, 2 Bridges Review, Soundings East, (b)OINK, Descansos Anthology, and Postcards Poems and Prose,* among others. He currently holds a BA in English from Westfield State University and will attend Western Washington University's MFA program in Fall 2017. He was invited to attend the Salem State Poetry Seminar and has worked with the Mass Poetry Festival in Salem, MA. He currently resides in New England in his parents' spare bedroom.